See with your Heart

- Brad Reel

Lake Michigan

POINT TO POINT

Todd & Brad Reed

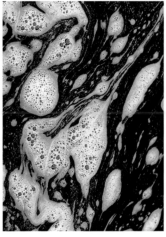

Sea Horse

DEDICATION

Dedicated to Martha Delite Benson (1903-1997), who saw the beauty in everything.

Burst of Life

Martha Delite Benson, Todd's grandmother and Brad's great grandmother, was fond of saying, "Thank you for sharing your valuable time." Todd and Brad thank you for sharing your valuable time with them as you view their artwork, read their stories, and share **Lake Michigan Point to Point** with friends.

I love Lake Michigan. Whether beating me up on a Coast Guard motor lifeboat, inundating my camera with a rogue wave or mesmerizing me with a mirror sunset, I love her.

I first came to know her as a young boy on Sunday drives and beach picnics with my parents. Mostly I saw her softer side in those days as I played on her beaches and swam in her waters on summer afternoons. During high school and college I came to know her more powerful side while salmon fishing out of Ludington on my parents' small boat.

I came to know Lake Michigan intimately after joining the Coast Guard Reserve in 1971. I have plied across the lake when the water lay mirrored like glass, and I have battled towering seas that turned the water into roiling, raging mountains. I have saved lives and seen lives lost. The Great Lake has instilled in me a profound respect and awe for its beauty and powers.

I have shut down the engines of my Coast Guard rescue boat in the middle of Lake Michigan on a dead calm night and seen the stars so clearly that it was clear to me I had never really seen them before. Even though I had no camera, in my mind I can still see the mental pictures I made that night, and I am grateful for that.

As outdoor photographers, my son Brad and I live to see a great picture. It is the experience of seeing, that is most important. It would be wonderful to be able to trip the shutter on all of the pictures I see that excite me; life doesn't always allow that. But I am grateful God has given Brad and me the gift of seeing the world in pictures and I am thankful for the pictures we have made of God's beautiful world.

For a year, Brad and I scoured Lake Michigan and its tributaries from Big Point Sable to Little Point Sable for the pictures that show the beauty and personality of this glorious region while also reflecting the beauty and character of all of Lake Michigan. A great photographer, Clyde Butcher—often referred to as the Ansel Adams of the Florida Everglades—has recommended photographing the area you know best. We have lived with the Point to Point region of Lake Michigan in our front yard and its tributaries in our backyard all of our lives. We chose this region to photograph because we know it as well as anyone and because we love it as much as anyone.

Surf's Up

A fast-response Coast Guard rigid-hull-inflatable boat flies over the water on Lake Michigan off Ludington. -tr

Rough Riders

Like a tank on the water, Coast Guard Motor Lifeboat 44345 pounds through breaking surf. The self-righting rescue boat and her crews aided mariners in distress between Big and Little Sable Points for more than 35 years. -tr

I have been to other picturesque shoreline areas of the country, including Cape Cod and Nantucket. They are beautiful places, but in my mind's eye, Lake Michigan from Big Point Sable to Little Point Sable is an equal gem. The beauty of this region typifies the entire length of Michigan's magnificent western shoreline, with topographic treasures carved out by ancient glaciers and polished over time. The crown jewel is Lake Michigan. It reaches beyond the water's edge into the land's interior, where plants, forests, meadows, and streams nourish and recycle the lake's life force. I feel blessed to behold this Great Lake.

My first book, Ludington Point to Point, was a very personal journey. Although I was often accompanied by my wife Debbie, sons Willie, Tad and Brad, nephew Ryan, and our yellow lab Beamer, the photography in that book was mine alone. But along the way, my wife, sons and nephew helped me become a better photographer by encouraging me, supporting me, carrying my equipment, getting me out of bed even when my body wasn't up to it. Photography apparently rubbed off on them. All the boys soon took to carrying their own cameras and looking for their own photographic visions. Subsequently, Brad and Ryan became consumed by photography. With his camera, Ryan has gone on to tell the story of human suffering and need, particularly in the Sudan and other African nations.

Brad and I have chosen to tell the story of home. I have always felt that good photography is all about feeling—the ability of photographers to put their feelings about a subject into a picture. Our feelings about Lake Michigan from Point to Point are within these images; we hope that feeling comes through, whether you have lived here a lifetime or not yet discovered this special place. -Todd Reed/tr

I can't imagine a more visually rich setting than that which I experienced as a child as I traversed with my father the land and waters between Big Point Sable Lighthouse in Ludington State Park and Little Point Sable Lighthouse near Silver Lake. My dad, the photographer for our local newspaper **The Ludington Daily News**, was fortunately able to include his family in his work. My brothers and I traveled wherever Dad did throughout Mason and Oceana counties as he looked for photographs or covered special news events. We were excited to be allowed to carry his tripod or camera bag. I did not know it then, but I was learning to "see" photographs, even though I did not have a camera of my own.

It wasn't until college that I felt the itch to take my own photographs. I took one photography course for fun, where I received valuable instruction on photography basics. While I was in my junior year at Calvin College in Grand Rapids, my dad bought me my first professional single lens reflex 35mm camera and a tripod. Dad was preparing to start taking photographs for his first book, **Ludington Point to Point**, and he knew that if I had my own camera we could work together to each capture our own vision. This was an incredibly intense learning experience for which I will forever be grateful.

After college, I tried numerous diverse career paths, all of which left me feeling unsatisfied. A few years ago, the opportunity came to make a full-time job out of what was increasingly becoming my number one passion: the visual art of photography. My dad and I have combined our efforts and now we are both following our dreams.

My dad is one of my greatest teachers. One thing he has taught me, not just with words but by example, is that every artist must find his or her independent vision. Everyone sees the world differently. While I have strived to match my dad's technical and artistic skill, I have sought to define my own vision. For example, when we shoot together my dad masterfully captures the grand full landscape shots, while I seek pictures in more intimate scenes within ten feet of my lens.

I have endeavored to learn from many other great photographers as well. My cousin and best friend, Ryan Reed, found an interest in photography at about the same time I did. Ryan also credits my dad with helping him learn to "see." Ryan now has had an incredibly successful career as an independent photojournalist, spending much of his time covering social issues in Africa. Ryan not only has great vision, but he is also a technically superior photographer. I am fortunate that he loves to share his knowledge and expertise with me.

Whispering Sand

The few secluded areas of the Silver Lake Sand Dunes strongly resemble whispering desert hills. -br

Old Man in the Sea

A compelling aspect of visual art is that different people may look at the same image and see different things. While I was composing this photograph, I noticed that the rocks, seaweed, and water resembled the face of an old man. I named this photograph with the hope that my viewers would enjoy the same illusion. -br

I have been inspired and instructed by the work of great outdoor photographers like Jim Brandenburg and the late Galen Rowell. In his book *The Inner Game of Outdoor Photography*, Rowell states that photography is an action sport; to be a great photographer one must be willing to get physically involved with the scene. I believe that my years of playing soccer have helped me to physically chase the fast moving light along the Lake Michigan shoreline. Jim Brandenburg has inspired me with his strong passion for the subjects he photographs. That passion is one vital element which causes his photographs to transcend the barrier between good and great. My passion for Lake Michigan and the areas surrounding my home in Ludington continues to motivate me to express myself through my photographs.

I am grateful every day that my wife and I were blessed with families that taught us to truly love and value the outdoors. I hope that my photographs will enable me to pass on my love of nature to my future generations, and you to yours. -Brad Reed/br

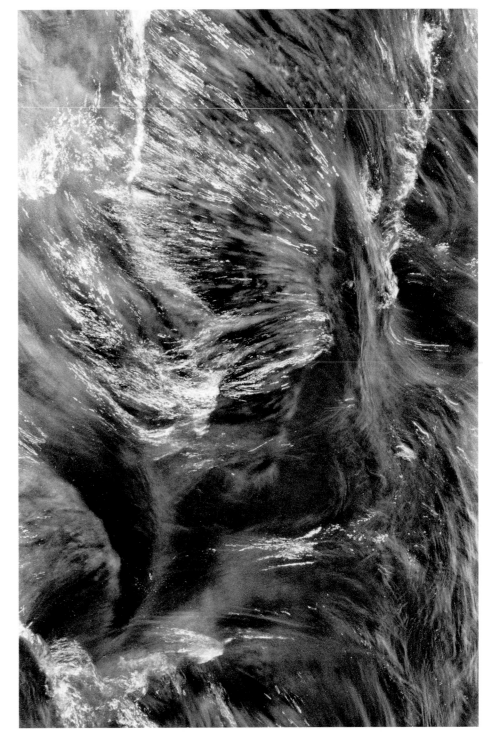

The Good Life   ⚓

*What is there about watching a seagull soar
into the sunset that makes us want to trade
places, if only for a short flight? I had that
feeling one warm, sunny evening while
watching this gull fly over Lake Michigan.
But I have witnessed the opposite extreme—
seagulls hunkering down on ice formations
against wind, snow and cold on subzero
mornings. Life as a seagull probably is seldom
romantic; often it is a fight for survival. -tr*

Angelic Wave   ⚓

*I have always enjoyed taking photographs
that may not feature identifiable subjects
but show the beautiful colors and patterns
that light creates on water. This photograph
was taken on the Lake Michigan shoreline
at sunset and is one of my favorites. -br*

Imagine

People who have not spent a lot of time along the Lake Michigan shoreline might find it hard to imagine that sunsets exploding with the most vivid color imaginable really do occur. Actually, the best color appears after the sun sets. Those who stay longer, relax and watch are often rewarded with a kaleidoscope of changing color. -tr

Midnight Sun

Of course there is no midnight sun in Michigan, but I could not resist naming this winter Lake Michigan shoreline image after the midsummer Arctic phenomenon. -br

On The Hook ⚓

For years, I have enjoyed observing sailboats swinging from their mooring buoys with the wind in the harbors along the Lake Michigan shoreline. This summer night in Ludington Harbor I watched the water and sky around a sailboat on the hook on Pere Marquette Lake transform from electric orange at sunset to shocking pink minutes later. -tr

Paradise ⚓

Every summer, my mom and family rent a cabin near an inlet on Hamlin Lake named Indian Pete Bayou. All year I look forward to spending time with the family around the campfire and photographing Hamlin Lake. My family and I have witnessed many great sunsets from this particular spot, but this was one of the best. -br

⚓ **A Sailors' Morning**

Some of my best photographs happen by accident. Before I took this photograph, I was struggling to compose a photograph of an abstract ice pattern below my feet. The shot was not working, so out of frustration I stood up and looked away. The tops of sailboat masts inside Snug Harbor Marina caught my eye. I casually snapped off one exposure and then went back to shooting the ice. Upon returning home to edit my work, I instantly knew that none of my ice photographs would go any farther than the editing table, but the sailboat masts were a sure winner. -br

⚓ **Black Beauty**

The sailboat Condor strikes a gorgeous pose even while high and dry on its cradle for the winter. The sleek C & C Redline 41 graces the waterfront of Pentwater, one of Lake Michigan's most picturesque harbors. -tr

Grand Sentinel

One of the best parts of my job is that I am always meeting new people. My wife, Betsy, my dad and I trekked to the Big Point Sable Lighthouse on a long summer evening. Upon arrival, we were greeted by volunteer lighthouse keepers working outside on the grounds. They generously offered to turn on all of the interior and exterior lights. My dad climbed a dune to shoot from the south, while Betsy and I walked down the beach a few hundred yards to shoot from the north. To our surprise, we found a perfect reflection of the lighthouse in a storm pool. This shot would not have been possible without the help of the lighthouse keepers and for that I am very grateful. -br

Big Sable Aglow

As darkness fell and the lights of Big Sable Lighthouse and the keeper's dwelling emerged, I was certain I was in the best spot to make the strongest picture possible of the famous landmark. I shot several dozen shots over a period of 45 minutes, when the cloud patterns added to the composition of the picture. But it was in the last few minutes of shooting that the electric lights and remaining light in the sky balanced the best. I packed up my gear, shouldered my tripod and strode excitedly down a big dune to meet up with my son Brad, whom I had lost sight of an hour ago. I showed him my "trophy" shot on my digital camera; then he showed me his. It was obvious that his was a Boone and Crocket "trophy" shot compared to mine. I was glad for his greater success but still exhilarated by my own visual experience and capture. -tr

Windswept

The first two weeks of October are a glorious time of year along the Lake Michigan shore-line. I tell my photography students more often than they want to hear, "Clouds are your friends." Early October is a great time to experience sunshine, fresh breeze and crisp, clear air painted with billowy clouds. When these conditions coexist, the dune grasses and beaches appear most alive. –tr

Storm Light ↔

Renowned National Geographic Photographer Sam Abell talks about learning to wait longer when he knows there is a picture to be made but all of the ingredients are not yet present. This October morning was the fifth consecu-tive morning I had driven 30 miles to Little Point Sable Lighthouse to shoot a scene I had composed on the first day. The light was sharp, the westerly wind was building up some great waves into repetitive patterns and the clouds looked powerful and stunning. I knew the final ingredient would be for one of the beams of light traveling between breaks in the moving clouds to fall upon the light-house. After 100 cold minutes, a bright beam appeared headed my way. As it hit the light-house I began shooting. A few seconds later the light also lit the dune grass in front of my camera and tripod. For about five seconds, one of the most glorious shoreline scenes I had ever witnessed lay before me. Then the magic light moved on and the scene became so much less moving. –tr

Christmas Light ⤙

A great challenge for my dad and me is to find new and creative ways to photograph the same subject. Fortunately, the ever-changing skies of the Lake Michigan shoreline work in our favor. On this morning, I had just captured the Little Sable Christmas Eve image and I was determined to find another beautiful photograph of the lighthouse. With the snow no longer falling, I waited for a fleeting moment of sunshine to illuminate the lighthouse against a stormy sky. -br

Little Sable Christmas Eve ⚓

On the morning of Christmas Eve, 1999, I was eager to try out the new camera that my dad had bought me for Christmas. He and I drove to one of our favorite places in the world, Little Point Sable Lighthouse. On the way, it began to snow unbelievably large, soft flakes. As soon as we arrived, I stepped out of the truck, set my camera on the tripod and took this photograph before the snow stopped falling. -br

Gold Rush

The magic light accompanying a rainbow turns dune grass to gold on an October morning along the Lake Michigan

shoreline. I have seen this dune on a thousand different days, but none more beautiful. -tr

Incredible Journey

*The Lake Michigan Carferry **Badger** passes beneath a rainbow on the same October morning I witnessed the other*

end of the same rainbow appear to land upon a golden dune near my home south of Ludington. -tr

Storm Warrior ⚓

*The Great Lakes freighter **Algorail** appears about to strike the Ludington North Breakwall during an autumn Northwester, but her veteran captain uses the powerful north wind and waves on her stern to his advantage. Moments after I recorded this scene, the ship's bow reached the pierheads, the wheelsman wheeled the ship hard to port, and she advanced ahead while her stern transferred swiftly to the south. The big ship guided into the harbor as though she were on a curved roller coaster track. It was a masterful piece of sailing. -tr*

White Squall ⚓

I have witnessed much larger waves but none more poetically perfect than this that surrounded the Ludington lighthouse during a February storm. My son Willie and I withstood a blinding snowstorm for hours before we were finally rewarded late in the day with a lull, and sunlight broke below the cloud ceiling to backlight the lighthouse and waves for a few precious minutes. -tr

↔ Lake Michigan Voyage

Steaming westward toward Wisconsin, the carferry **Badger** departs Ludington Harbor on one of her daily Lake Michigan crossings. The big ship carries passengers and autos back and forth between Michigan and Wisconsin from spring to fall in almost any kind of weather. -tr

Power and Light

On this stormy October night, the rushing waters of Lake Michigan, a large piece of limestone rock, and God's magic light created a powerful spectacle along the South Breakwall in Ludington. I got a little wet taking this photograph, but the reward was well worth it. -br

Impressions

Large waves washing a feather and stones up onto the Lake Michigan beach near Pentwater caught my eye as my older brother Tad and I were walking along the beach. I had to move quickly before the next crashing wave whisked the feather away. -br

Winter Watch

A Northwester churns up Lake Michigan, turning the lakeshore dunes into a sea of blowing snow. February days like this one make most people long for spring. I never want to miss a good Northwester any time of year. -tr

Breakers ⊕

Hurtling forth and plummeting down, breaking waves capable of overpowering almost anything in their path, rush toward the Lake Michigan shoreline. On this November day, no one and no vessel dared to challenge them. -tr

Gale Force ⚓

Wind contorts my face, waves roar and crash just short of the feet of my tripod, sun gleams and dances across the water, clouds paint the sky, I am in my glory. This is as good as it gets for a Lake Michigan photographer. These are the days I dream about and rarely experience. This is one of the best moments of my life. My camera records it so I and others can experience it again and again. -tr

Sea of Confusion ⚓

Southwester waves rush at the Ludington South Breakwall while others rebound off them, creating confused seas—a condition sailors like to avoid when the waves get this big. Changing colors faster than a chameleon, this sea and sky would soon become blood red. -tr

Red Sea ⚓

More red than the Red Sea, Lake Michigan changes color like a lava lamp in the red light of a September sunset afterglow. This scene presented itself only seven minutes after the "Sea of Confusion" scene. -tr

Sunburst

As I hustled to find a vantage point to capture this image, I was struck with an overwhelming sense of calmness. I realized that

I was one of only a handful of people at that moment lucky enough to witness the perfect blending of a human creation and

God's creation. This was a defining moment in my life when I knew I had found my calling as a photographer. -br

Pentwater Sunburst

An hour or two before sunset, my dad can usually foretell whether the sky will produce great color. I have endeavored to

learn this skill from him. On this evening, my dad and I both noticed that the sky looked very similar to four nights earlier

when I photographed the particle ray behind the Ludington North Pier. We immediately drove to Pentwater and our predictions

were realized. -br

Ultra Violet Light ↤↦

A valuable composition lesson I have learned from my dad is that visually small objects, or "added ingredients" can make or break the image. On this evening, the person strolling down the breakwall and the seagulls circling the Ludington North Pier conveyed a summertime mood. Without these "added ingredients" the image would not be complete. -br

Dueling Lighthouses ⚓

Pentwater's North and South Piers fight for viewers' attention during a spring sunset. The crowning moment came as the setting sun dipped into Lake Michigan. -br

Breezy Night

Many of my summer evenings in Ludington are spent with family and friends. I had not shot any photographs for a few days, so on this evening, my wife, Betsy, and I politely excused ourselves from a family gathering and drove to the First Curve at the Ludington State Park. A delicate blade of dune grass first caught my eye. I lay down on my stomach and started shooting. Summer's hectic pace seemed to freeze for an instant. -br

Great Blue ⚓

I have learned hundreds of photography hints from my dad, but one of the most important things he has taught me is that the sky often displays the best color about twenty minutes after sunset. I had just captured the Breezy Night photograph when Betsy and I drove further into Ludington State Park to look for more photographs. As we passed over the Sable River Bridge, Betsy noticed a heron in the water below. I grabbed my gear and I was off. To get the best photograph possible, I knew I would have to get in the river. Not wanting to threaten or disturb the heron, I waded ever so slowly to within fifteen yards of the bird, and quietly captured the photograph I was looking for. Thanks for the helpful hints, Dad. -br

God Beam ⊬

Heaven knows how many times a God beam like this one has lit the Ludington Lighthouse. When I saw the sky open and the light pour down, I quickly maneuvered my small boat close to the light, lay over the gunwale, and fired away for about 20 glorious seconds before the clouds and spotlight moved on. -tr

Cobalt ⚓

Among the most amazing nights on Lake Michigan are those when the color in the sky refuses to diminish even when the viewer's mind says it is too dark to be so vivid. I could no longer see the camera controls on this night when the sea and sky turned black and blue. -tr

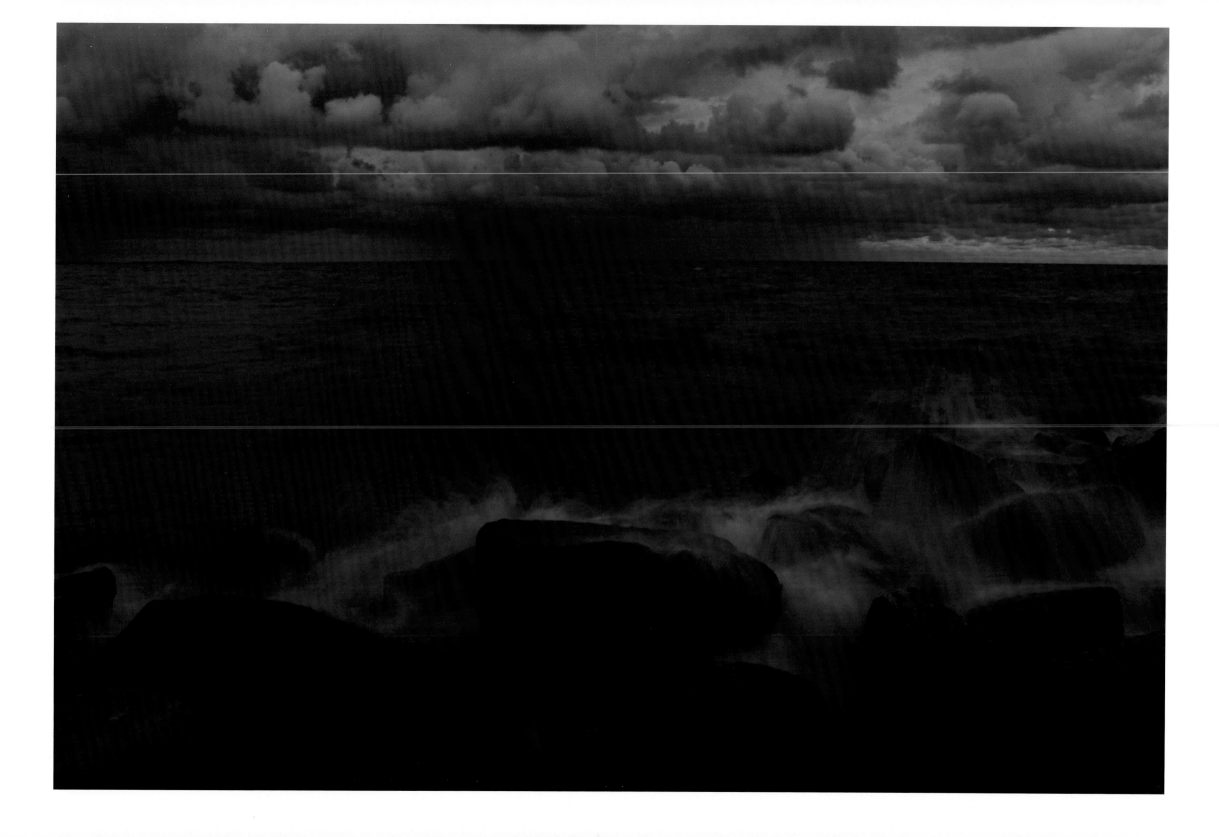

God's Light   ⟷

At least once more in my lifetime I would like the privilege of photographing a moment as power-packed as this one I witnessed in September 1997. I was as charged as the air about me as an enormous storm cloud fired lightning bolts faster than a giant Gattling gun and swept across Lake Michigan toward my vantage point on the Ludington shoreline.
I believe recording this magnificent moment was God's will. We named it "God's Light." -tr

Roil Blue   ⚓

roil (v.) *To be in a state of turbulence or agitation.*

Seas roiling like a cauldron of churning, boiling water are bathed in storm light during one of the most spectacular Lake Michigan gales of November I have ever seen. Gulls soar above the Ludington Lighthouse, on the lookout for fish churned with the waves. -tr

Glorious ↤

Epworth, located just north of Ludington, is beautiful every day of the year. The large hillside, with a scattering of majestic old homes, makes for wonderful photographs. -br

Morning at the Beach ⚓

Being there, just being there to patiently watch the rising sun first strike the tips of the dune grass and then slowly paint more of the grass is a mesmerizing experience. On this October morning, a pink sky finished the Lake Michigan Shoreline painting. -tr

Summer Curves

Sea, shore and sky abound with more curves than a curvaceous woman. S-curve shapes have been pleasing the eye of artists and art lovers for centuries. An August sunset afterglow highlights the clouds and meandering Lake Michigan shoreline between Ludington and Pentwater. -tr

Channel View

Tranquil summer evenings on the Lake Michigan waterfront lure boats and people like fish to water. This late July evening in Pentwater was no exception. As in so many other favorite locations along the Lake Michigan shoreline, people and their vessels are drawn back year after year like salmon to their birthplaces. -tr

Moon Over Ludington ↦

I love the coldest mornings; they often render Lake Michigan waterfront scenes in incredibly sharp and colorful ways. The setting moon and rising steam made this a picture that warmed my soul. I live for moments like this when my camera takes me where my heart wants to go. I tell my photo students, "follow your heart with your camera." -tr

Breathtaking ⚓

The night took my breath away, not from trying to breathe the below zero air but from viewing the icy splendor before me on Lake Michigan at Ludington. -tr

Snow Sculpture ⚓

Victim of an eroding Lake Michigan shoreline, a tree uprooted years earlier is transformed into a snow sculpture on a dune at Epworth Heights north of Ludington. Finding scenes like this along the Lake Michigan shoreline confirms for me why I am a winter person. Winter is a photographer's friend. -tr

On Ice ⚓

Like a coating of white feathers, frost decorates sumac branches on a dune overlooking the Sauble River Outlet at Ludington State Park. This February scene is the polar opposite of those hot summer days when the Lake Michigan tributary and its banks abound with swimmers and sunbathers. Sauble River Outlet is one of the most picturesque spots on Lake Michigan in any season. -tr

Dune Masterpiece

The Silver Lake Sand Dunes are home to many good times and great memories for thousands of people. You can feel the energy that the bustling atmosphere produces. If you wander long enough, you can find areas on the dunes that look as if they have been untouched by humans for hundreds of years. When I was photographing this scene I was amazed at the apparent lack of human presence. It was not until I gave this photograph to my grandma, Bev Marble, for Christmas, that I was aware of the litter present in the scene. -br

Guiding Light

Many of our photographs are long time exposures that are shot on a tripod. We use long exposures because we photograph well after the sun sets below the horizon. This was a 30-second exposure, at f-stop 3.3, and at 100 ISO. -br

Dew Drops ⚓

After capturing the Pere Marquette Sunrise
photograph, I put my dad's "twice as close"
rule into effect. With every shot I moved closer
to the river until I reached the water's edge,
where I could go no further. This scene caught
my eye because of the dew drops suspended
from the tips of each blade of grass. My next
mission was to position myself so that the
blades of grass fit perfectly into the reflection
of the clouds on the river. -br

Pere Marquette Sunrise ⚓

I abruptly awoke one Sunday morning at
five A.M. and could not get a haunting
image of the Pere Marquette River out of my
mind. I was positive that if I ventured out to
our property and stood in the exact location
I had envisioned, I would see a beautiful
sunrise. I shot out of bed and was on my
way. I guess you could say I got bit by the
photo bug in my sleep. -br

Summer at
Hamlin Lake ⚓

*The sun has set, the boat traffic has died
down. It is a quieter time on Hamlin Lake,
a time to savor the beauty of one of the most
popular lakes connected to Lake Michigan. -tr*

Sun Ride ⚓

*Like cowboys riding into the sunset, bicyclists
ride toward the sun on the Ludington waterfront on a splendid September evening. -tr*

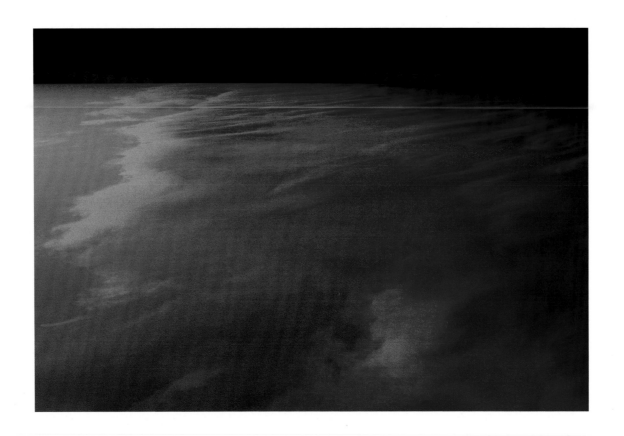

Storm Front ⊥

Batten down the hatches! Storm clouds tumbling mixer-style steamroll threateningly ashore along the Lake Michigan shoreline on a June afternoon. This scene and the "Hot Pink" scene are among the hundreds of spec-tacular big sky views I have witnessed from my home near the Lake Michigan shoreline south of Ludington. They reflect the similar amazing scenes that unfold frequently all along the shores of Lake Michigan. -tr

Hot Pink ↔

The proof is in the pudding! The Ludington, Michigan area has been proclaimed by several national publications as one of the best places in America to view a sunset. This sunset after-glow confirms their findings. -tr

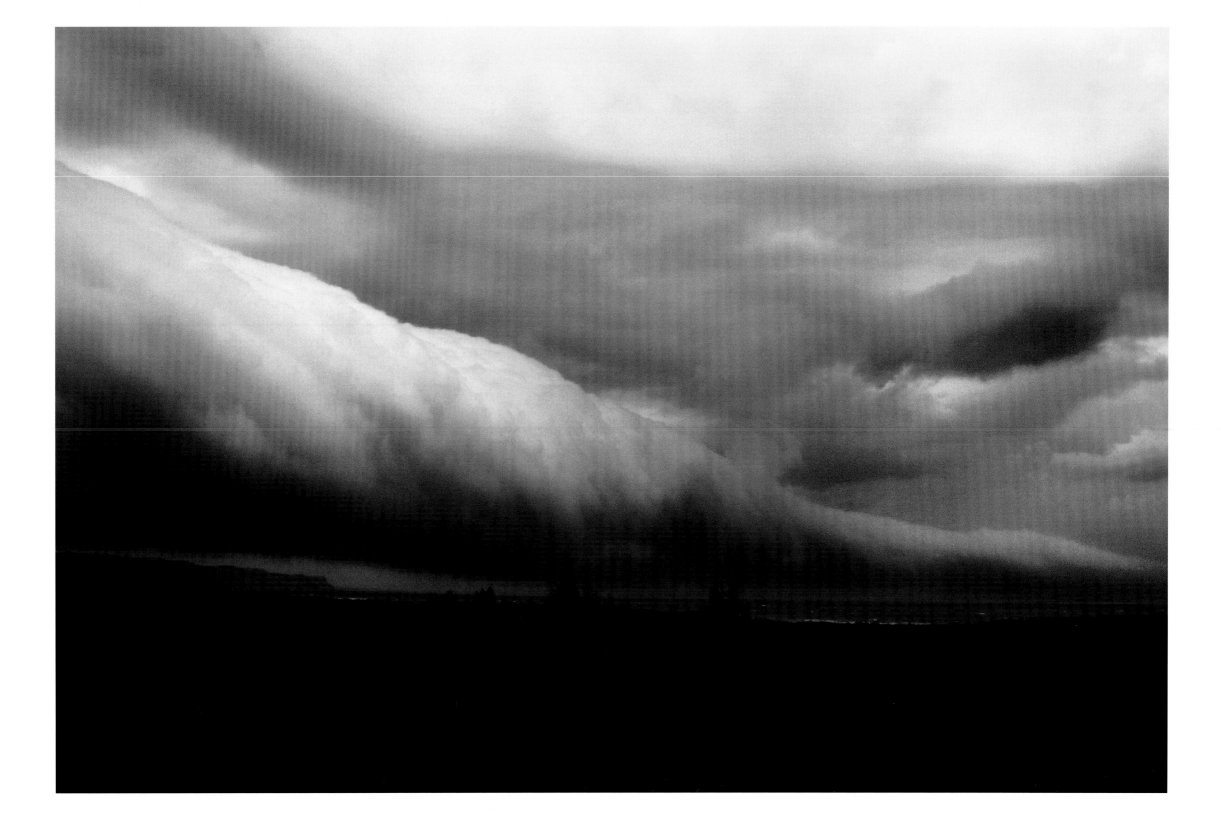

Color Purple ⚓

A wild flower fights for space in a colorful sea of purple loosestrife—an invasive species which, despite all its beauty, threatens indigenous plant growth in the Pere Marquette River marsh and other wetlands connected to Lake Michigan. I must admit, I would hate not seeing its annual return. -tr

Stealth Standout ⚓

A great blue heron stands watch like a statue while fishing along a bank of the Pere Marquette River south of Ludington. Purple loosestrife colors the river marsh. The Pere Marquette, designated by Congress as a National Wild and Scenic River, helps provide Pere Marquette Lake and Lake Michigan with its lifeblood—water. -tr

Luminous ⚓

Growing up, I spent many hours along the Lincoln River banks with my older brother, Tad, and my uncle, Rod Marble. This photograph was taken while we were on one of our early spring adventures. -br

Iris ⚓

I made this picture on the Island Trails in the Ludington State Park. The bright blue areas of the photograph are Hamlin Lake. My father-in-law, Don Verduin, and I spent a great deal of time trying to find the perfect wild iris to photograph. Don actually found this flower first and was kind enough to let me in on his treasure. -br

Unfurling Fern ↔

*When bright sunlight hits water, it creates
a wonderful array of sparkles. When those
sparkles are photographed, the aperture ring
inside the lens makes them appear as perfect
geometric shapes. I feel that the sparkles
make this photograph a stronger image. -br*

Green Lagoon ⚓

*There are numerous small swamps and lagoons
between Big Point Sable Lighthouse and Little
Point Sable Lighthouse. They are always home
to interesting wildlife and wonderful colors.
In other words, a photographer's paradise. -br*

The Three Sisters

On the Western shores of Bass Lake, near Pentwater, three large tree-covered hills grace the horizon. I have heard many

names for these hills, but the local favorite is The Three Sisters. -br

Riveting

I keep trying to edit this picture out. I enjoyed making the picture of the riveted keel of a rental boat on the Hamlin Lake

shoreline at Ludington State Park. I like the resulting image, yet I did not feel comfortable with including it in this book.

My son and shooting partner, Brad, loves the image. He sees abstract pictures almost everywhere he looks and shoots

many of them. Getting out of your comfort zone can be uncomfortably good. So the picture stays. -tr

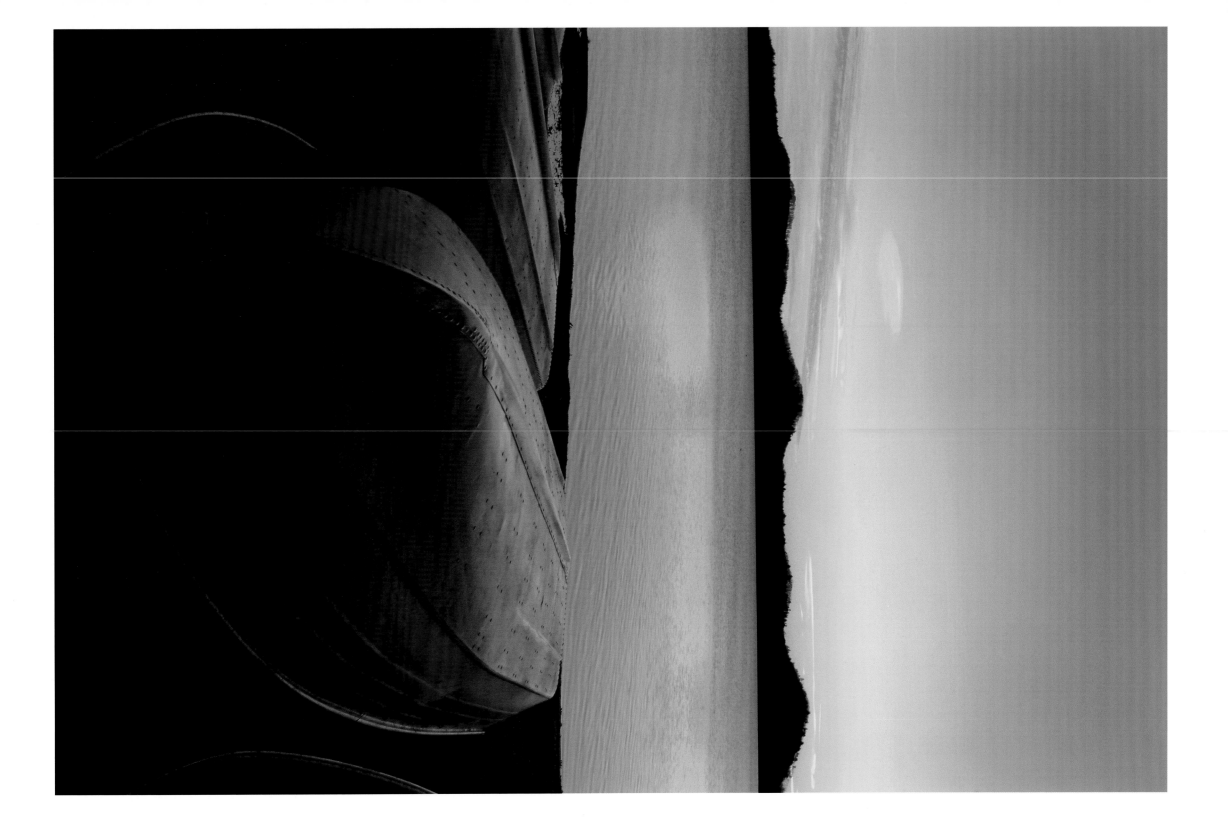

Eye of the Storm ⚓

I have a passion for photographing ice.
The abstract shapes and the contrast of
tones make for great images. I discovered
this scene along the Lake Michigan shoreline
in the middle of February. It is one of my
favorite photographs. -br

Autumn Gem ↔

Floating lazily down the Sauble River toward
Lake Michigan, a maple leaf drifts over rocky
shallows. They say good things happen to
those who wait: finding a good backdrop
and waiting for the subject to come into it
is relaxing and often rewarding. -tr

Big Lake Buck ⚓

Autumn along the Lake Michigan shoreline is a quieter time, a good time for spotting wildlife. On a November morning, this buck appeared along the high clay banks south of Ludington, in an area where no hunting is allowed. –tr

October Appearance ↔

Sometimes it seems like we wait forever for the leaves to turn along the shores of the inland lakes tied to Lake Michigan. Then, seemingly overnight, a glorious change greets us on a morning like this one on Hamlin Lake. My son Brad and I encountered this fleeting scene at Victory Park on Upper Hamlin Lake in mid-October. Brad was still running with tripod and camera for a different vantage point while I made this picture along the park waterfront. Fortunately, I got off one shot before a cloud dropped the curtain on the fall color light show. –tr

The Beach House ⚓

Every summer, thousands of visitors frequent the Beach House, inside Ludington State Park. Weddings, family reunions, and eating ice cream are just a few of the uses for this grand structure. -br

Glass Lake ⚓

Bass Lake mirrors its famous landmarks, the Three Sisters hills that separate this lake from Lake Michigan north of Pentwater. A pontoon boat lies motionless at its offshore mooring. -tr

Tropical Illusion

When I am not working at one of our galleries or taking photographs, I can often be found at the soccer field. As my cousin Ryan and I pulled into the Sterns Park beach in Ludington for a cool-down swim after a few hours of soccer, I noticed a vibrant orange streak of light dancing on the water. Knowing how fast light can change, I did not risk taking time to remove my shin guards and soccer cleats. I ran down to the water's edge and captured the reflections just in time. Needless to say, I got a lot of strange looks as I was photographing that evening. -br

Turquoise Moon

For a few precious minutes, the light of the rising sun and the sunlight reflected from the setting moon balance on an April morning along the Lake Michigan shoreline between Ludington and Pentwater. Sunrise beach walks bring me alive as I watch the world about me come to life. -tr

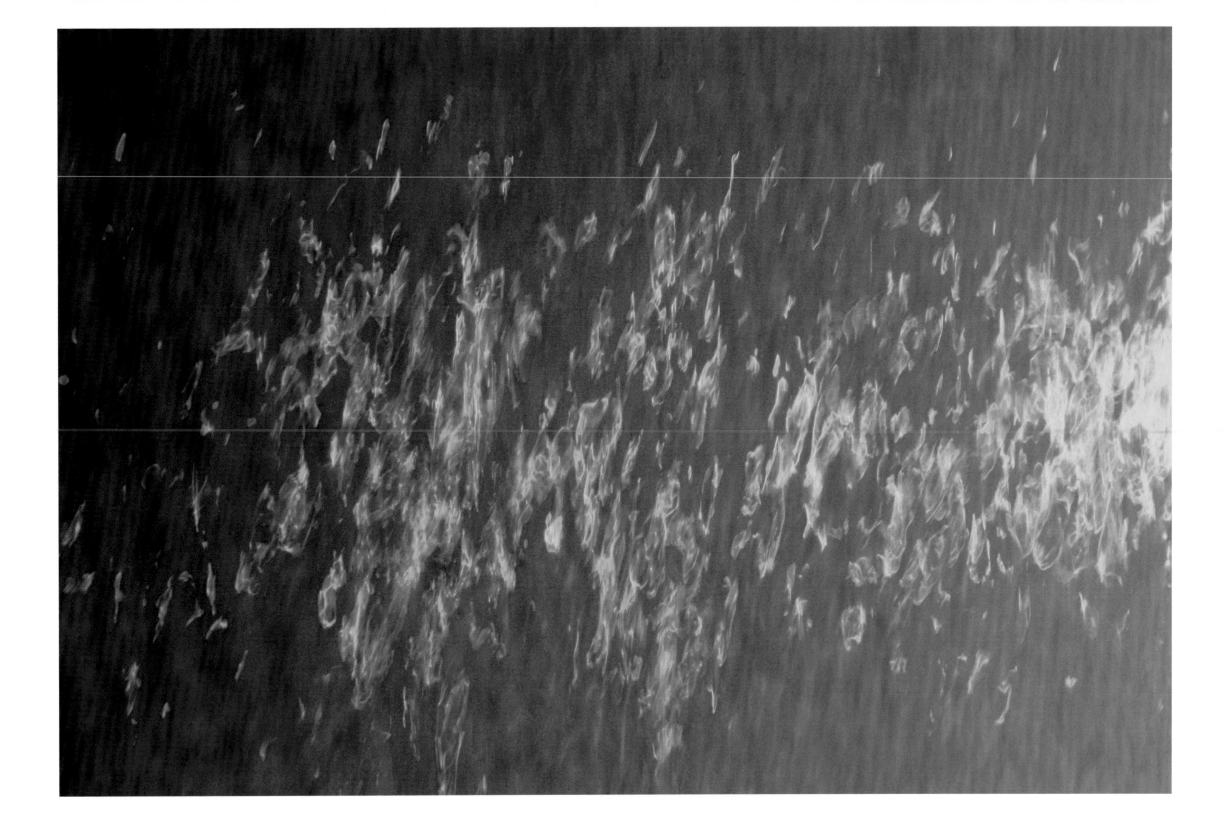

Still Waters ⊬

As steam rose from the still waters of Silver Lake, the sun peeked over the trees and illuminated the scene before me. I captured this image early in the morning before the daily barrage of boaters flocked to their playground. -br

Silver Lake Serenity ⚓

I have been known to do crazy things to get a photograph. On this occasion, I was frustrated because I could not position myself to capture this sailboat and its reflection, yet omit the other boats from the scene. I had two options; climb a tree alongside the road, or stand on the roof of my car. My car still has a large dent in the roof. -br

Summer Time Fun ⚓

Calm, windless nights on Lake Michigan may not make for great sailing, but they sure do make for sensational photographs. -br

Reflections of Summer ⚓

My dad has taught me how to use my camera to convey different emotions within the same scene. To portray a peaceful summer evening mood, I stood in the puddle and positioned my camera and tripod inches above the water's surface. The angle resulted in a mirror-like reflection of the sky and clouds. I also set my shutter speed to 15 seconds to make the water appear more like a painter's palette of colors than a cloudy storm pool. -br

Heavenly Sunrise ⚓

*As I stood in one spot on the edge of
Lincoln Lake for over 40 minutes, the sky
produced three dramatic color changes.
The first display was bright pink with the
rising sun. It quickly changed to ruddy-
orange and gradually finished with blue-
purple. This was my only photograph of
that morning that showed the large rays
of light shooting toward the heavens. -br*

Outlet Outlook ⚓

*August looked more like October when I
crested a dune to find this view of the Bass
Lake Dam, the Outlet, and Lake Michigan.
Like so many small outlets along the Lake
Michigan shoreline, the Bass Lake Outlet
follows the path of least resistance to the
big lake. That path shifts with changing
winds and seas. -tr*

Valentine's Light ↕

After leaving a Valentine's Day fund-raiser in Pentwater, my wife, Betsy, and I headed North to Onekama to eat at a favorite restaurant, The Blue Slipper. As we drove, the winter evening light began to cast a hot pink glow on everything in sight. I begged Betsy to allow me a few minutes to shoot. I ran through snow deep in my dress pants just in time to capture the Valentine's light before the sun set below the horizon. We were a little late for dinner and I was wet and cold, but it was worth it. -br

Big Sky ↔

Few places on Earth offer as grand a view of the sky as the east shore of Lake Michigan. Hikers on the Ludington South Breakwater provide a sense of scale to show the size of storm front clouds arriving in Michigan from Wisconsin. -tr

Snowball ↦

A mute swan cruises the Sauble River near its outlet to Lake Michigan on a winter afternoon. Waterfowl flock to the river in winter to find open water. Bird watchers and photographers also flock there. -tr

Blue Bayou ⚓

A bayou along the Seven Islands Trail at Ludington State Park turns as blue as the sky on a September evening. The Seven Islands Trail is a treasure trove of beautiful settings. Magic light transforms the view into an extraordinary one. -tr

Splash ⇥

Thoughts of a refreshing Lake Michigan swim surface while watching waves splash amidst some rocks on a late September morning. A reality check tells me the water temperature is probably barely above 50 degrees Fahrenheit. I decide to stick with making a picture of the fresh water. -tr

Ice Mountain ⚓

Rugged ice and towering waves define the Lake Michigan shoreline in the coldest winter months. On cold, clear days when the sun graces us with its presence, the ice displays different shades of blue and white. On this day, my friend, Rob Alway, and I made our way out on the ice and we each came away with some powerful photographs. -br

Withstanding the Storm

My dad and I have taken many beautiful photographs at the end of Ludington Avenue. On rough days, that location allows you an unobstructed view of the Ludington North Breakwater, while still offering some protection from the blowing sand and water. One risk still present is thin ice. Just after I captured this photograph, the ice beneath me gave way. Luckily, only my feet got wet. -br

Fire Water

On fire with the light of the setting sun, waves explode like fireworks against rocks lining the Ludington South Breakwater. Lake Michigan's energy never ceases to amaze and excite me. -tr

Ice Blue Railing ⚓

Stopped temporarily in its track by ice pushed by westerly winds across Lake Michigan into Ludington Harbor, the carferry *Badger* is framed by an ice-coated railing along the Ludington Harbor channel. This scene and the "Red Tug" scene unfolded during the 1980s when the sturdy ship still carried railroad cars and operated year-around. –tr

Red Tug ↔

The tugboat *John Henry* circles the *Badger* to help the 410-foot carferry battle its way out of Ludington Harbor against wind-driven ice packed tight from surface to lake bottom. This scene and the "Ice Blue Railing" scene are my favorite winter pictures of all time. I knew, as *National Geographic* photographer Sam Abell might say, that I was "in the presence of a picture." –tr

The Captain ⊢→

Since I was a young child, I have been fascinated by the carferries and other large ships that traffic Ludington Harbor. This statue of a mariner stands tall and proud, very much like the ship captains I have been privileged to know. -br

Teeth of the Storm ⚓

As I lay on my stomach at the end of the inner North Breakwater, an icy cold wave crashed over my head. I braced myself for the cold shock and pressed the shutter button at the same time. It all happened so fast that I was not sure if I captured the moment. I continued to lie in the snow and shoot, but another wave never came. Fortunately, my first shot turned out. -br

Holy Water　　　⊶

Each night that I step onto the shores of Lake Michigan, I am amazed by the unique light show that unveils itself. No two sunsets are the same. Just when you think you have seen them all, Mother Nature renders a refreshingly new display of her beauty. -br

Fire and Ice　　　⚓

Jagged icicles in the foreground create a unique look at the Lake Michigan shoreline. The ice formation changed before my eyes with each powerful wave that pummeled the shore. -br

Light Ship ⚓

Displaying more lights than a Christmas tree, the carferry **Badger** stays very alive even while docked in Ludington Harbor between Lake Michigan crossings. The coal-fired steamship carries passengers and automobiles between Michigan and Wisconsin. -tr

Lighting The Way ⚓

The Algorail, a frequent visitor to the Ludington Harbor, used two powerful spot-lights to guide herself quietly into port. I set my camera to 800 ISO in order to stop the ship's motion in this low-light scene. -br

Point Guard ⊢⊣

Big Point Sable Lighthouse guides mariners safely past its treacherous shallows as it has since 1867. The famous landmark stands guard at the north end of a C-shaped 35-mile stretch of Lake Michigan shoreline that meanders from Big Point Sable to Little Point Sable. Big Point's tower rises 112 feet from its base to the top of the lamphouse. -tr

Little Sable Moon Light ⚓

The moon setting in the West and the sun rising in the East created an extraordinary light show before my eyes at the Little Point Sable Lighthouse. The lighthouse has illuminated the most westerly point of land in the lower peninsula of Michigan since it was built in 1874. Little Point Sable Lighthouse is one of only a few brick lighthouses in Michigan still operating. -br

ACKNOWLEDGMENTS

We want to thank all the people who made **Lake Michigan Point to Point** possible, including everyone we met on our journeys while photographing this book.

We owe a special debt of gratitude to the following:

Debbie Reed, for years of work building our business and her continuing support and love for us.

Betsy Reed, for her keen skills as a text editor and other help in making this project possible, and most of all for her love and support.

Tad Reed, and all the other men and women who serve our country.

Willie Reed, for helping to build a strong foundation for our business.

Ryan Reed (ryanspencerreed.com), who pushes all photographers to get outside their comfort zone.

Kay Marble, Brad's mom and hero, for showing him that with hard work and determination, dreams can come true.

Bud and Dorothy Reed, for unwavering support and encouragement.

Budde Reed, for his business expertise and sound advice.

Our entire family and all of our friends.

Greg Dunn (digimagery.com), for keeping this book digitally on track and for his friendship and teaching ability.

John Gouin (graphikitchen.com), who helped with the fine tuning of the book's layout.

Rob Alway (alwayphotography.com), for his friendship and professional support.

Scott Blasco (scottblasco.com), for composing the music for our book slide show.

Carl Sams and Jean Stoick (carlsams.com), for sharing their professional knowledge.

Jim Goulet and the staff at Ludington Photo Center—Todd & Brad Reed Photo Gallery.

Bert and Cheri Petri and the staff at Our Gallery (ourgallery-petri.com), for making us feel at home in Pentwater.

Artists Market (ludingtonartistsmarket.com), and **The Wooden Gallery** (woodengallery.com), for matting and framing the artwork in our galleries.

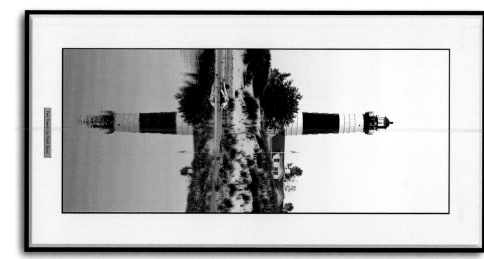

INFORMATION

To order prints from **Lake Michigan Point to Point**, please call Todd & Brad Reed Photo Galleries at 231-843-0777.

You can also order prints and books, learn about our photography workshops, and view hundreds of our photographs at **www.toddandbradreed.com**.

Prints are available matted, unmatted, and framed.

We look forward to you stopping by one of our galleries in Ludington, Michigan, or Pentwater, Michigan, to view our artwork, visit with us, and show us your photographs.

Feel free to write us at:

Todd & Brad Reed Photography
114 West Ludington Avenue
Ludington, MI 49431

www.toddandbradreed.com

Blue Moon

Published by Todd & Brad Reed Photography, LLC.
114 W. Ludington Avenue, Ludington, Michigan 49431
231-843-0777

Photography & Text ©2005 by Todd & Brad Reed

Individual prints of the photographs in this book are available for purchase directly
from Todd & Brad Reed Photography.
*Visit our web site at **www.toddandbradreed.com**. Or call 231-843-0777.*

Library of Congress Control Number: 2005900990

ISBN 0-9765528-0-9

10 9 8 7 6 5 4 3 2 1

First Edition
First Printing, April 2005

Printed and bound in Canada, by Friesens of Altona, Manitoba

Designed by Todd & Brad Reed in conjunction
with Digital Imagery and Graphikitchen.